# Roots

by Grace Hansen

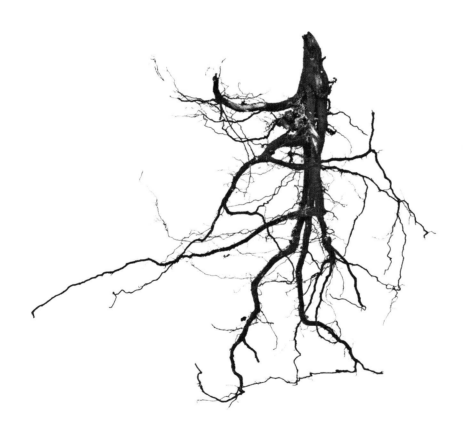

Abdo
PLANT ANATOMY
Kids

**abdopublishing.com**

Published by Abdo Kids, a division of ABDO, PO Box 398166, Minneapolis, Minnesota 55439.

Copyright © 2016 by Abdo Consulting Group, Inc. International copyrights reserved in all countries. No part of this book may be reproduced in any form without written permission from the publisher.

Printed in the United States of America, North Mankato, Minnesota.

102015

012016

 THIS BOOK CONTAINS RECYCLED MATERIALS

Photo Credits: iStock, Science Source, Shutterstock

Production Contributors: Teddy Borth, Jennie Forsberg, Grace Hansen

Design Contributors: Laura Mitchell, Dorothy Toth

Library of Congress Control Number: 2015942106

Cataloging-in-Publication Data

Hansen, Grace.

 Roots / Grace Hansen.

  p. cm. -- (Plant anatomy)

ISBN 978-1-68080-138-5 (lib. bdg.)

Includes index.

1. Roots (Botany)--Juvenile literature.   I. Title.

575.5/4--dc23

2015942106

# Table of Contents

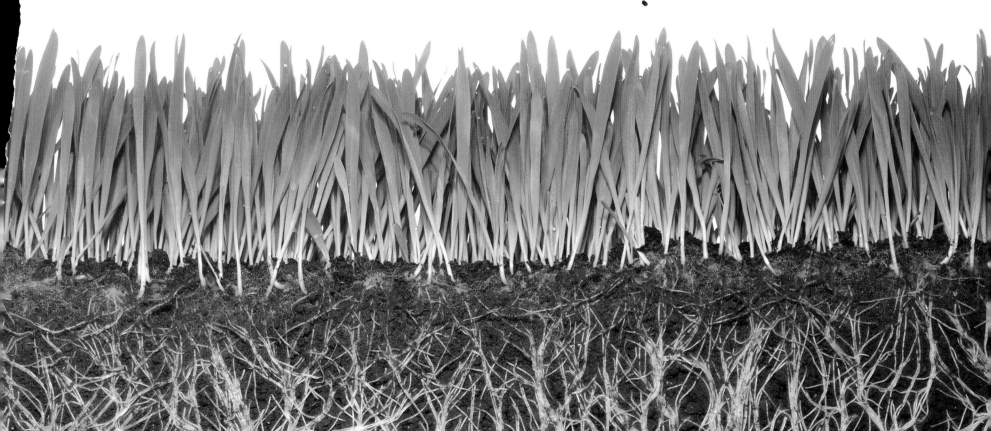

## Roots First!

Roots are the first things

to grow from seeds.

They grow downward.

4

5

## A Root's Job

Roots bring food and water to plants. Plants need these to live and grow.

Roots do more than help plants grow! They **anchor** plants into the soil.

9

Roots are important to soil, too. They drain water from the soil. This keeps soil from being too wet.

10

11

Roots help keep soil in place.

This prevents **erosion**.

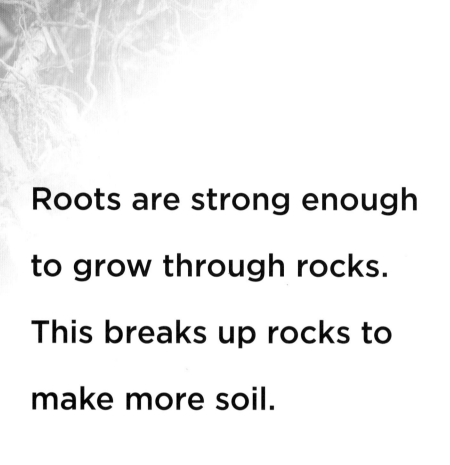

Roots are strong enough to grow through rocks. This breaks up rocks to make more soil.

14

15

## Kinds of Roots

There are three main kinds of roots. There are **fibrous roots**. Grasses have these roots.

There are **taproots**.

Carrots have these roots.

19

Some plants also have

**adventitious roots**.

These roots can grow

from stems and leaves.

20

# Root Systems

**adventitious root
corn plant**

**fibrous root
chrysanthemum plant**

**taproot
garden beet**

22

# Glossary

**adventitious roots** – roots that grow from stems and other plant parts to provide extra support for a plant.

**anchor** – something that holds an object in place.

**erosion** – the gradual destruction of something by natural forces such as wind and water.

**fibrous root** – a root that branches out in all directions.

**taproot** – a primary root that grows downward and gives off small lateral roots.

# Index

# abdokids.com

Use this code to log on to abdokids.com and access crafts, games, videos, and more!

Abdo Kids Code:
PRK1385